NARCISSUS
DREAMING

Also by Dabney Stuart

NARCISSUS

DREAMING

POEMS BY

DABNEY STUART

1990
LOUISIANA STATE UNIVERSITY PRESS
Baton Rouge and London

Copyright © 1981, 1983, 1984, 1985, 1986, 1987, 1988, 1989, 1990
   by Dabney Stuart
Manufactured in the United States of America
First printing
99 98 97 96 95 94 93 92 91 90   5 4 3 2 1

Designer: Laura Roubique Gleason
Typeface: Bembo
Typesetter: G&S Typesetters, Inc.
Printer and binder: Thomson-Shore, Inc.

LIBRARY OF CONGRESS CATALOGING-IN-PUBLICATION DATA

Stuart, Dabney, 1937–
   Narcissus dreaming : poems / by Dabney Stuart.
      p.   cm.
   ISBN 0-8071-1591-6 (alk. paper). — ISBN 0-8071-1592-4
(pbk. : alk. paper)
      I. Title.
PS3569.T8N37   1990
811'.54—dc20   90-5745
                                            CIP
Grateful acknowledgment is made to the following publications, in which
some of these poems originally appeared: *Balcones, Chronicles, College English,
Harvard Magazine, Inlet, The Journal, New Virginia Review, Oxford Magazine,
Panhandler, Poetry Miscellany, Poetry Northwest, Prairie Schooner, Quarterly West,
Southern Poetry Review,* and *Zone 3.* "The Man in the Black Bear" and "Moving
Pictures" first appeared in *Chelsea.* "The End of the Century" was originally
published in *Gettysburg Review* (1988) and is reprinted by permission of
Gettysburg Review. "Hidden Meanings" is reprinted from *Massachusetts Review,*
The Massachusetts Review, Inc. © 1985. "Getting What She Wants," "One
Woman, Seen Twice," and "Gospel Singer" first appeared in *Southern Review.*

I am grateful to Washington and Lee University for a John M. Glenn Grant,
which supported me in the composition of some of these poems.

Publication of this book has been supported by a grant from the National
Endowment for the Arts in Washington, D.C., a federal agency.

CONTENTS

for Sandra
and for Bill McDonough

ONE

The Long Goodbye

Their faces are still there
on the inside of my eyelids
where I put them—
projections on a screen,
nebulae in the rich dark.
They turn toward me, turn
away. A bald, grief-slagged
head tries to dissolve
but its weight persists, forming
a pain no other shape fits.
A thin fog leaks from a corner
of its mouth, what it has left
of speech. Another with hooded eyes
swims in itself, prenatal,
the promise of its will no more
than driftwood in burred sand.
A third puts on an expression
of great knowledge it doesn't know
what to make of. It tries to smile
through all that perplexity,
becoming a lugu-
brious mo-
lecular entangle-
ment in end-over-end slow
motion, a child's hour-
glass filled with many-colored
grains of glass suspended in honey.

I sleep through them all.
In the little dark I make we are
a galaxy of affection, turning
in the sweet curves of space.

The End of the Century

To beguile the time, look like the time.
                                    Macbeth

A salamander sidles
from a tree limb, meanders along
a patio eave, drops casually
onto the pale apples from France
nestled in the wicker
basket beside their bed.
The air is thin, cool.
It's too early to sweat
but neither lover asprawl
on the aqua sheets moves;
only the salamander's wry
tongue ruffles the still life.
                        Later,
the odor of gin and citrus
will mingle with sunburnt
sex and dried sawgrass.
The day will thicken, seeded
with the very habits they have
slept so deeply to outgrow.
Their skins will dry even
further, peel. It will become
possible to imagine their lips,
painted lush crimson against
the backdrop of cloud
and sky, mouthing aimlessly
in mid-air: they round sumptuous
vowels, sip lime rickeys
through designer straws, kiss
nothing, enact
a language before the bodies
of their sound are born.

On the Air

The woman in red spreads her legs
and practices television.
She doesn't exercise exactly, or dance.
Her performance goes nowhere, has
neither theme nor focus; its knots
and slides, lapses and thrusts
create no rhythm, build to nothing.
It's like an episode
of Phil Donahue in pantomime,
tuned to itself, articulating nothing
beyond the only word that matters, *Watch.*
When she finally parts
herself as if to say *There's more,*
and more to me than anything
you could imagine when I'm gone
her mouth opens, a thin
sizzling emerges from its corner,
fills her head and neck, zigzags black
and white along the thorax, through pelvis
and bicep and thigh, frying her.
The small dot of light where she was
disappears only a little faster
than its image in the pupil of my eye.

The Other Woman

My brother brings home
yet another girl. She awakens
my lust, my gut burns
with it, my peritoneum becomes
a tapestry of fire. I want to wind
myself into her until I am so lost
the Garden of Eden could retire.
I stare at her. Together
we could bring happiness
to the orphans of war.
I start to say hello
but our mother enters
wanting to know which
of us has brought her
the new mirror.

Getting What She Wants

Motion of the most ordinary kind
Across ice, or any opaque surface,
Renders the skater's body self-satisfied,
Tunes it until no expectation
Hovers beyond the next demanding stride,
Anonymous as the flight of a bullet;

Various designs, one covering
Another, may mark the ice, the skater's figure
Rehearsing the groove it rides, continuous,
Needing only to keep moving, describing,
Especially when the surface thins to nothing:
You step out onto the bottomless air of your life.

No One Told Me It Would
Be This Way

Arlene Dahl and Alan Ladd were true
to each other from take one to the last
slow fade of silver. Neither intrigue
nor war nor economic disaster unsettled
their sweet confinement. But now
she folds blankets for the Salvation
Army and he works
the graveyard shift in an elevator shoe
factory in another city. At night
she takes the subway across town
to a high-rise apartment she shares
with two anthropologists from Nairobi,
while he jogs two blocks to a Victorian
tenement fifth-floor walk-up
where the pipes knock erratically
in his sleep. They dream predictably.
From a balcony she looks down on the Fargo
tables, nods to the bartender, fondles
her detachable beauty spot. Alan rides
the rigging of a quinquireme bound
for Madagascar and the Improbable Straits.
About 3 a.m. in February they meet
in a diner on the inner coast of Maryland
and over coffee and crabcakes talk softly
of the past, the early mists on the surf,
the end of nothing which hadn't already
ended before the lights went up.

Surface Tension

Beside the pool, lounging
in summer, she browns, her flesh taking on
a sleek luster, like a ripe pear's
in a centerpiece. Her attention seems to fall
on the flat metallic blue, wrinkling slightly,

which a body breaks with its lean intrusion,
the water cupping, making a brief peak,
becoming again the sun-shot skin she watches.
Or doesn't watch. It's hard to tell,

as if the nictating membrane were still
there on her eye, closing without closing,
sparing her the grit and pollen of normal air,
letting her sleep through everything

with her eyes open.

Swinging on the First Pitch

You go up there cocked.
You don't care if the whole
stadium knows you're hitting away.
After all, he's been bringing
the first one in from the start.
There's no need to look
it over. It's the same stuff
you've been taking all day, all
season, since you can remember.
So what if the two of you keep
leading the league in strikeouts,
at least this time he's not getting
ahead of you while you stand there
taking up space. Anybody
can do that, that's what other people
buy tickets for.
If he doesn't groove it, you're sure
it'll be in the strike zone,
or near, and the way you feel
it could be a mile off and you'd still
go with it, dump it down the line
for a double. You're ready
for anything he's got, dug in, rippling
the air, wrists rolling smooth
in the box ready
for anything.
He goes into his motion—
the same old cunnythumb herkyjerk
sidesaddle nonsense, nothing
up his sleeve but what you've known
is there all along—winds,
delivers. It's a fast ball,
big as a globe, 110
miles an hour, coming
right at your head.

Franz Kafka Applies for a Literary Fellowship

1.

My plans are uncertain.
I would like to finish something.
I would like to know
which dream to wake from.
And into.

2.

If awarded this grant
I will burn the money
to write by. The light
will cast the shadow
of my pen on the wall
behind my head. I will call
the work, tentatively,
The Foundation.

3.

I am not requesting
a travel allowance.
I don't expect to move.
One false word
and the bridge might collapse,
or the train arrive
at the wrong station.
This would inconvenience many people.

4.

I won't try to remember anything.
A heavyset man
standing in his bed
looming
has promised me
he will attend to that.
He tells me
this will save him a great deal
of trouble, and relieve him
of much grief.

5.

A peripheral effect
of little consequence
which might weigh in my favor:
all of Magritte's bowlers
will be my father's.

6.

My happiness does not depend
on the success of this application.
Therefore, it is incomplete.

Gospel Singer

He doesn't touch
the microphone, but the way
he stands plays
on its uprightness. He is
singing about being
closer to God than ever
before, about walking
the valleys with Jesus,
about what life has
in store. His left
side between his belt
and his armpit is drawn
tight like the top
of a drawstring bag.
His denim work
shirt, forced into this small
compass, crumples
a thousandfold. His chin
drives into his left
shoulder, a fiddler
with no fiddle. His right
side is stretched
slightly—you can imagine
a bow beginning
to bend. Everything
rides on his bringing
his mouth down to the mike,
almost into it. It is more
than intimate. He delivers
his part
with such control
you hear nothing
but music, as if
he were breathing
song. When the last
harmonic fades
and the other musicians'
hands glide in slow motion
past their final
licks,
         he straightens,

disfiguring himself back
to normal, smiling
sheepishly, as if
there'd never been any good
news to bear
into the world,
to hang there singing.

Audition

for Darren

Nothing is
as transient as sound.
Voices
come in at the ear,
rise up in the mind.

A brief white moth
hazards its way
through foot-high corn.
A sensitive ear
follows its patterned
flight by the soft beat
its wings leave on the air.

So a song flies blind,
and the singer with it,
having only the mind's
fine trace in the ear
for his voice to follow
out to the blank air.

And then it's over. And over.
A light sleeper—
say one whose infant pain
of mucous-clogged ears
that wouldn't drain
echoes a ground beat still
under his thickening years
too deep to make flight of—

hums to himself
the white moth's
untraceable sweet
lost wake, and so mutes
his own ineffable
longing for still air.

TWO

One Woman, Seen Twice

1.

She kneels, washing her hair
in a pool of the same color.
There is no reflection. Above her
a butterfly seems to disappear.

2.

She squats, moving her hands
in the riffling stream.
Across from her image in the water
a butterfly dances on the air.

Somewhere in her mind
her life shimmers, reflected there
like her face in the stream,
herself in the middle,

hands in the water,
water through the hands.

The Girl at the Pool

Curved like the warm vacancies of dreams,
Ordinary beyond belief, she strokes the water
Naturally as a leaf descends through air,
Renewing her own grace, keeping the pressure going.
Anyone can do this she seems to be saying:
Difficulty is the mind's invention,

Happiness the body's, which simply *moves*.
If she's right, she's even more desirable, being
Lovelier than the thought that made her up.
Bent in the midnight toward one shifting word
Eliciting another, do you ever see her
Rise from the pool, dripping, and walk toward you,
Renewing your vision of the implausible prize:
Your lover, your daughter, your wife?

The Secret

She whispers it
to me behind her hand.
Her breath

is warm and moist
like a fresh fig split
open

in the sun. No one
would guess she is still
alive. I hear

her as if we were
both young again, before
the playground

swings or the dark cedars
of our first
kiss. She

gives me back
a ring, gold,
set with my birth-

stone. I see myself
throw it beyond
her, into the sun,

and turn
away, blinded. She
touches my

wrist, again
whispers. Her voice
becomes

a compress over
my eyes. She says
everything

I forget, except
Welcome home,
forever.

The Next Step

If one sets aside the standard schlock
of the usual science-fiction thriller—
the sensory overload, the pseudo-shocks,
every mercenary's ideal arsenal,
and the impossible Saturday
afternoon serial cliffhanger
superchick episodes of self-rescue—
what's left?
                    Well,
imagine deepest interstellar space
—the measureless, starstruck void—
incarnate as a female creature
about the size of a wholesale bargain warehouse.
She is the Causeless Cause,
the Great Egg-Layer whose endless rows
of infertile ellipsoid modules need,
in order to peel open, flowerlike, and hatch,
only a series of warm-bodies, proximate
hosts in which to clone themselves.
Hence, human intergalactic travel.
The spaceship's crew enters her
dark maw and stands upright.
They reach the murky acreage
of her ribcage and tentacled abdomen,
exploring from the inside
the Universe as Mother and Mother
Fucker in one. It's the next step
after the black widow and the praying
mantis—not to devour the male
when he's served his purpose,
but to dispense with him altogether.
A double birth, from egg and host,
and no need for a father. After the cloning
produces creature number two, the host,
in its spun glass casing, conveniently explodes.
Presumably the progeny, magnificently
dentured, go on to live forever.
                              This is,
of course, the evil nightmare we are saved from
by the real dream that issues from it:

the macho heroine perpetuates herself
by having a daughter

without sexual intercourse, pregnancy,
labor or nurture, discovering her instead
holed up in an air-duct complex
in the Great Mother's warehouse body
and womb, orphaned and already schooled
in cunning, independence and survival.
She saves her
from the monstrous process noted above,
and they live happily ever after,
but not totally alone.
The extended family consists
of half an android and a one-eyed
mutilated ex-corporal who,
in an earlier reel, had taught Mom
to operate a high-tech flame
thrower and a breechsplit grenade
gun. In the end
they lay themselves down to sleep
peacefully in their cocoons of frost.

Umpire

for my daughter

He learns to imagine
the vertical shaft of air
hanging above home, to hear
its inaudible hum
when pitches he can't see
tick its corners.
Under the lights, when
the humidity is right, it becomes
prismatic, shimmering
with the curve's kiss,
the slider's slick dive.
Sometimes, after calling
one perfect, pivoting,
driving his right arm out
and back in a groove smooth
as a piston's, he looks away

over the green swath toward
the lights, seeming to carry
that brightness in his eyes.
If he could hold it
there all
the time no one would
argue with him,
no distorted faces writhe
Hydralike into his, no benches
clear. Everyone would see
how his vision was the strike
zone—brilliant, impeccable,

fair. And the earth is flat,
and, next spring, bull-
frogs in Bradenton will
sprout wings. Still
he lets his mind wander
briefly inside that aura,
touching the certain borders
of his calling, his peaceful dream.
Then he edges back out of it,
watches the bright air disperse,

Moving Pictures

1.

The man in the overheated
trenchcoat is following
the lamplit young woman,
rapidly mincing. Shots
of his feet, her feet,
a raddle of fenceposts,
slurred. Her ticking
footsteps counterpoint his
wingtips' thick, methodical
plod. Tight
skirt. Drawn
jaw. This much could be
a still life, futureless—
an emblem of the wanton
poise between our lust
for abandonment and our fear
of it—were it not
for the rumpled figure
in the next block, off screen,
waiting. He mashes
his cigarette under his shoe,
exhales thinly, hunches
his jacket against the cold.
What we expect him to do
seems obvious—rescue
the faint of heart, bring
the bully to justice, simplify
desire. Instead, he calls
into the dark, his voice
intimate, promising, replete
with the untold past, its
loss and longing. The footsteps
cease, the camera slides
toward mist and slippery
light, nebulous as space.
There are three of them
now, left with themselves,
with life, not taking sides.

2.

But what if the young
woman, her neck lightened
softly, wanted to turn, be
taken, left trashed
in the rumpled alley, wanted
that scene's endless
repetition—luxury without
blood, mother and son
in their least recognized
dream arrested. What if
the man off screen isn't
there at all, run off
with some woman in another
script. What wretched
torment waits for the two
of them, exempted
even from chagrin, forever
planning suppers of cold
cuts and dried fruit,
the drab, high-ceilinged house
echoing their silence.
Cobwebs, dust, twilight.
Each evening they rise
to the same occasion, walk
through it, as if rehearsing
for the morning's session
of therapy on the worn couch.
The man off screen has grown
a short beard, reappears, listens
aloofly from his chair, falls
asleep in the old story's
facility, its deadly rut.
He is luckier
than the audience, which has
long since turned to its own
version of such nonsense,
its own unwritten dreams.

3.

Suppose the camera
lies. He is
not

following her,
nor is she fleeing
him. They are

participants in a game
whose rules
lie

outside their frame
of action, their
still lives spliced

together, even beyond
the ribbons of film cut simply
because they didn't

fit. They have
heard the story in part
two, and have agreed

to reserve
comment. Perhaps
that is what they are

fleeing together,
the parts we
would reel them

up in, their endless
recognition
of the fanatic

light projecting
through our eyes
them, their only

roles.

Serials, 1947

Saturday's hero finds it easy
to manage waking each morning
with the sear of blue steel in his gut,
a dizzy rod of white neon
running from temple to temple
behind his eyes, easy
to burn with July in February
when the thick fold of green
blooms in his pocket, and nylon
tricot amulets dry lazily
on the shower rod. *Desire*
is one thing   he thinks, lying
in bed under the slow ceiling
fan or waxing his mahogany
propellor before takeoff   *my desire*
another. It lifts me beyond
the cockpit, the sponsor's word;
whatever my body does
while it dies, while it's dying
lives. He rescues
the semimaculate woman
bound in her last ditch, takes off
again under the twined sag
of a swinging bridge, dusts the treetops
with his shadow under radar, makes
his slipstream tremble in the wild
blue, yonder. He's heading
home for the smoky gambit,
the husky voice in the tavern
seeking to slip into the next tableau.
Whatever his next breathtaking
death, he knows it will be
undone: when the plot recovers again
next week he'll be meeting
himself here, raising his glass
in the long mirror back of the bar.

The Fourth Dimension

It was the wrong dream.
A black regatta throbbed
against the clinking of lime
tonics, rum drifted
alike from tongue and pen.
Women of dubious content
poured their stories into the blue
bilge, wanting only
the time to elucidate, to revise.
Everyone wanted to believe
nothing in the past
had really happened, it was just
memory. When the sails
shifted as if by rote, no one
on deck slid with the tilt;
no matter what
wind might rise or wave
slaver the hull, the future
was flat and their shoes were
nailed to it. A canopy
billowed. Sighed. Subsided.
He had wanted the sheets
to ride him forever; this
windless drift unnerved,
set him aside. *Some other
time, some other set
of masts against the skull*
a voice under the dream muttered,
neither waking nor sleeping,
a voice he had
heard echo his best
wishes before—
a puzzle, a prayer.

THREE

Knowledge Is Power

My mother the judge keeps
her cigar going while the angels
of birth appeal for me.
The ash lengthens slowly, the cigar's
incredible imitation of itself,
its second nature, until,
after forty years, the angels'
plea for mercy begins to fade
into a garbled whispering, then silence.
They watch the growing ash;
their mouths take the shape of zeroes
as if they, too, a kind of choir,
would smoke, and stare down
from the bench vacantly at tomorrow,
and postpone the verdict.
                              *I should know
better,* I think, but I know nothing.
Such sweet pleasure spreads
through my veins that I smile, and bring
my hands together; it is as if Queen
Isabella has granted me my ships.
I clap for everything—my old lady,
her strenuous inertia, the heavenly
chorus stunned in tableau with her, my
self standing there clapping,
releasing—everything. *This may have
taken a lifetime,* I think, and bow,
and turn away toward the new landfalls
I don't even know are there.

Narcissus Dreaming

He's still standing in
the boat after all
these years, his rod
angled absently outward,
the toes of one foot
nested in an oarlock.
He might be getting ready
to step out over
the side, but there's nowhere
to go. Seems
like old times. Among the vague
ripples wrinkling
his reflection, the cork
bobs, settled
where his liquid belt
buckle shimmers, waves.
His attention all
but dissolved, the bait
long since merged
with that image the surface
keeps, suddenly
in a depth as far
from himself as he is,
something pulls. Going
through the motions
he pulls back. Bob, line,
sinker, hook return
to him, bringing
his reflection off the water
as if it were a laid-out suit
of clothes lifted
by its center. He lowers
it into the boat, takes
it upon himself,
drenched, obscene,
a perfectly imperfect fit,
leaving the water
imageless, opaque,
other.

My Children Going

It isn't even interesting.
It's the underside of the underdog
in the muck, in the end.

I tie tin cans to my tail, try
to roust the neighborhood at three
in the morning, but the streets
stay hollow—it must be the same
dream everybody's dreaming.

The music of the spheres.

Dark enough for you? a voice says.
Never seen the like of it the same voice
answers. *You can't tell
that crazy man's rattling
in your sleep from your sleep
from laughter half the time,*

can't tell it from the air I breathe.

2.

*You ought to see somebody
about that* Perry Mason says, easing
from behind a neighbor's hedge.
He cuts through our usual nightmare
pleasantries to tell me the news
is bad. *All the sleek
anchors are melting
at their desks* he says. *What's left
of their invented faces, hearts, drips
down their stools into the grates
in the floor beneath them.* He tells me
how camera crews quit, associate
producers panic. *Under
the blitzklieg spotlights' pitiless
glare* he says *Brokaw blurs. Rather
ripples. Their thick residue clogs
the drains. The Union of Newsroom Grease
Trap Cleaners is on strike
and the studios are filling up.
Test patterns crowd the screens again,*

the center cannot hold,
the season of terror is upon us.

His lone and level voice drones lovingly
on, soothing my soul no matter what
its tragic load. I tell him
his fly's undone. *Sign of the times*
he says, turning to leave.
                                                    Wait
I call to him. *What about my children?*
Talk about transformation, talk
about change! Those anonymous
tadpole-shaped possibilities I flooded
their mothers with
have grown into birds
which accomplish exotic migrations
more swiftly and with less design
than light moves
on the face of the waters.
                                        They molt
monthly; they flash me
their iridescent names
in falling feathers. I'm up
to my knees in who they were,
their castoff guises, not even my own
memories of them.

He doesn't listen. He lumbers off
toward reruns, toward his sequel
as Della Street's incestuous father,
the small screen rhapsody
he's always dreamed of,
bringing it all back, venting
the old office and late-night dinner
frustrations, acting out the taboos.

3.

This must be part of the real
life I promised myself some years
back, seeing them transformed
into what no one could tell
they already were
then

becoming. Gills, genes,
feathers—stranger mutations
have burgeoned in the midnight
muck, the dark dazzle
of apparent loss drawing out of itself
forward into love, walking
on air.

Doing Nothing

If it would only rise suddenly
into the air of its own weight,
like a trans-world balloon brilliantly
stitched together of rainbow,
I would scramble in
and stand there up to my waist
in nothing, lifted in nothing by
the invisible air I don't think about
breathing, not bothering to turn
my head, letting the balloon turn
and sway on the music of nothing;
except for heating the gas, I
would be hardly there, or not
there with myself, letting it ride.

But it's another old lie's tale
I feed myself in the early morning,
trying to steal another half
hour's sleep before I go down
to the basement and settle in,
picking up the awl, seeing again
the pie strips of canvas radiant
around me, dun to the edges of doom,
the plastic rushes tied in bundles
like kindling against the wall
next to the furnace. The awl
has a pleasant heft, a friendly worn
place where in odd moments of dis-
traction I rub my thumb across it.
When I'm working well, stitching
in a slow, commensurate daze,
the needle warms, making a coarse,
haphazard music I'm learning
to hum to myself.

The Cabbage in History

If I stink
while I'm cooking, I'll be good
like Rasputin and limburger.
If you bury me
in the shallow earth
in a sealed crock
I will become so vile
only the delicate
gourmets of the Orient—
who also eat dog
and worship the past—
will find me
delectable. I can wrap
the ground imagination
of the Middle East in one
leaf, a gesture
as modest as God
riding into Jerusalem
on an ass. Only my cousin
the turnip shoulders
the world with less pomp,
only the onion hugs
itself more tightly. Without me
the collected sermons of Puritan
New England would have died
in the orifices of Mather,
of Edwards, odorless and
cold. Even now I am seducing
shoppers from the East
coast to the Rockies;
I boil in ten million pots.
The soft smell
of decay nuzzles Woonsocket
and Yazoo City, Eldorado
and St. Cloud, drifts lovingly
toward Melville, Alamogordo,
Cortez. No one is
safe from my implacable
aplomb, my zest.
I am headed
for the Pacific.

The Blurb Writer

In one year on the back
of 26 books his name appeared
under paragraphs he rarely
remembered writing. In some
cases he couldn't recall
the book's author, or the book either.
Yet there they were—the books
scattered on his desk, a table,
the floor—covered with his indisputable
words, and his name under them
like an egg they had laid.
It *was* his name.
He recognized it.
But he felt as if it had escaped
him, gone off on its own,
performed those blurbs like obscene
dances, and then stretched out
prostrate beneath them, exhausted—
or, like a party balloon suddenly
untied, gone skitting
randomly, inscribing paragraphs
of air, beneath which it lay at last,
shriveled, deflated, spent.
Was this what it meant
to be a name? he wondered.
That was what he'd wanted,
aimed for, lain prostrate himself
at the feet of other names to achieve.
The blurbs themselves, when he read
them, mercifully blurred,
glared back at him
like so much birdshit on a windshield.
He had just enough perspective
left to wonder at the curiosity
it would take to push someone
past them into the books they crusted.
This is death he thought. *I have
created death,* and he saw
his blurbs rising like mushroom
clouds, carrying their sickness
into the atmosphere forever.

His fearless name huddled
beneath them, never giving up,
still trying to leave
its sign on the world.

Love Story

Everywhere I turn, your broken leg
Dances, by itself, white cast shimmering.
I dare the light, ask for the next strut, but
Tenderly hear *There's no future in it,*
Honey, it's an illusion: the audience

Laughs when the lights show me, the stage, empty.
Only *your* leg could get away with this,
Give a command performance in a dream
And fleece the dreamer. I leave them laughing—
Nevermind the reviews, it's your leg I care about.

Somewhere it leads over the rainbow me
High and hairy; the brilliance of no gold
Every equaled its luminosity.
Paradise is next, I think when the signatures
Peel off and fly away—*the cast pristine!*
Applause subsides. So, everything subsides.
Relax said middle age when I woke up,
Dreams are for those who never heal. We healed.

The Harpist's Dream

The strings of her instrument become
saplings, the bark just coarse enough
to abrade her fingers as she strums.
They begin to bleed a little.
She nuzzles the roughening curve
closer into her neck, but still can reach
only the fourth tree, the rest stretching
out in a row in front of her
all the way
to the end where the mirror is.
She's down there, too, reaching
for herself. In this forest
the animals could be music
if she knew how
to make the saplings hum,
but all she gets for her effort
is more
blood. Pressing, she wants
to grow into the harp, to feel her neck
and shoulder thickening, her hair
twining upwards toward the lower
boughs, her fingers settling
into the striated rivulets of bark.
Once upon a time
she might have managed
to finish this escape
—merging with the harp trees
swaying, played by the wind—
but now she finds babies growing
on the limbs, raw, newborn
babies, bald as ice, their mouths
voiceless zeroes. One by one
she lifts her fingers to them, touching
their lips with her little blood
along the whole scale of their astonishment.
When she wakes, they begin to sing.

My Hostess at the Renovated Inn

for Tom and Shirley Ziegler

When I say her hair was alive
I don't mean to suggest Medusa.
I mean no gel or spray
had frozen the living strands
into that carveable sadness
manikins wear. It swayed.
It flowed. Put me in mind
of an underwater dancer, a dive
so deep and long breathing and drowning
become dreams of each other.
Her eyes sang, too, not a mark on them.
But you could have skated on her
apricot lip gloss, and her forearms!—
her right one lunged into a tunnel
of frisky bracelets, her left throbbed
in the coils of a brass snake.
I wanted to shake hands
for the music's sake, wanted
the apple she was, wanted to be myself
devoured, I didn't care by whom
as long as we were the whole
story.
        When she descended
the curved staircase it was no deb's
entrance. She moved
the way I dream my mother
might have moved if she hadn't been
my mother.
        She was the perfect
stranger of my heart, nameless,
moving aimlessly through the great
hall, receiving, now and then
smiling through the sheen.

When she left through the screened
door into the shadows of the porch
it seemed just right, entrance and exit,
a brilliant rift in the days'
ordinary drift and muddle, a might-have-been
as clearly marked as a fairy tale.

But as I smoothed my pants
and floated toward dinner, no more
than a customer again, she came back,
hipping the screened door open,
hoisting by one of its rungs
a ladder-backed chair like a jug
of moonshine over her left elbow,
cradling in her right arm two small
dogs, hairy, all squirm and yip.
She climbed the stairs, bumping
the ornate banister, adjusting
the dogs, rising askew along that curve
of burnished cherry, disappearing
at last, leaving a spike-heeled shoe
tilted against a riser. I stood there,
wondering if all such gifts
are inadvertent, so lonely given.
Though I seemed rooted
to the floor, and the ground
under it, my next step, going
nowhere, was curiously light.

Hidden Meanings

for Bob Denham

Both Hansel and Jack hated their mothers:
Jack sold the old cow
so she threw his seeds away;
Hansel let his feel his fingers a lot
and then stuffed her in the oven.
Their fathers were troublesome, too:
one was a wimp willing to sacrifice
his children; the other was so big
he had to be cut down, stalk first.
We know nothing about Rumpelstiltskin's
parents, but he played by himself in the woods
and when he couldn't get a baby by proxy
stuck his wooden leg through the floor.
The two boys finally got rich, like Cinderella,
but beyond that the ends are obscure.
Maybe they entered life, and found it to be
its own magic fable, as consequential
as any *Snow White Blood Red,*
and on the surface, true.

FOUR

Bearings

One reason it took him so long
to wake into his best
dreaming was how tightly
he was wrapped in the cocoon
his mother.
                He
had, after all, distended
her svelte belly beyond retreat.
After she spewed him out
she thought it only
fitting she
should carry on in the style
he had accustomed her to.
Wasn't life itself no more
than finely spun armor one
learned to move in without
breaking? He could learn;
she would live twice.
                    Trouble
was, the inward being
felt its first birth's deep
rehearsal so bone-incurred
it did the whole
routine again: kicked,
rebutted, pummeled, stretched,
recoiled, encouraged,
writhed, contested, rolled
and rerolled. Sometimes he placed
his hand on this growing, feeling
his stranger worming itself
alive, a slow smile spreading
through him—blood

in the veins, sun in the skin—
his heart become a minor
organ for the while it took
this ordinary
parting to happen in. He

carries traces of the afterbirth
still: little fissures
he drifts toward in the mind, snags;
random flecks on the brightening wings.

Victorian Bobbysox

In the whorehouse parlor
the women mill
around in their pastel
sweaters and pleated skirts.
One's hair twines into plaits,
another adjusts her barrette,

another half twirls, making
her skirt rise, then twist
against her thighs, resettle.
The ruffled curtains
stir.

When the music stops
desire takes its place
in the air. The whores
and their men glide through it—
paired, dreamy, in-
accessible—answering a faint
necessity no one really
needs, disguised,
redressed.

They begin to file back
and forth through doorways hung
with beads, repeating
themselves as if the supply
were infinite,

while a man who arrived
late watches them look
alike and turn under
the lintels, and turn
into his mother, and the shadow
of his mother.

Nothing seems to
prevent him from raising
his hand, calling
a name to the one
and only everyone his longing
would ride forever,

but he waits, refusing
to be taken in, until
the whole show gradually
shrinks, retaining its perfect
scale, becoming
no bigger than a wind-up
carousel, spinning,
tinkling, stunned.

He places it on the faded
glow of the player
piano. As he leaves
he slides his hand absently
along the edge
of the circular stool.
In the empty
spaces, diminished at long
last into their toy
time, it, too, spins.

Bean Ball

for Sid Coulling

It looms toward me
like one of those mystical orbs
in a Spielberg movie. There's no time
to duck, or shrink
my shoulder inward, so I unbutton
the flap on my hip pocket,
reach in and grab
my all-purpose anti-bean-ball kit.
I unfold it and extract
a number-nine needle with the ease
of Arthur pulling Excalibur
from its stone. For the merest
shimmer of an instant the ball
poises on the tip of that needle,
a chrysalis. Then pure
impact, shuddering
the axis of the world.
The errant pitch explodes
into innumerable spheres the size
of baseballs. Brilliant
with surprise, their crimson
seams spinning like crazy, they ride
the crowd's humming elation
skyward, creating
a new concept in domed stadia.
Under their lightening
the pitcher and I take hands,
lift them high between us
and circle the bases together
with the winning run.

The Man in the Black Bear

Where have ye been? Behind
What curtain were ye hid from me so long?
—Thomas Traherne

The man in the black bear
coat can't sing a note,
has hair in his mouth,
thinks growls are speech.
He calls me *chickenshit*
when, at two years old, I run
from the gaping folds
of his great black hide.
To him it's a joke, a way
of growing me into the real world
of men and animals lying
in wait for each other.   He keeps
surprising me when I open
new closets, turn corners from one
year into another, ascend stairs
from this house to that house.
His caustic flapping spreads
its sudden gulf in front
of me, waves; his grunting
echoes down time's deep-
throated tube, until, at 50,
my spell-muted little
self turns up in my arms,
shivering, his mouth sprung open—
a hole deep enough to fall into
forever. *What took me so long*
to get here? I wonder, losing
my balance. The bastard's been dead
a decade, the bear
he lived in gone to moth-eaten
shreds before the war ended.
How deep can a scouring voice go
anyway, calling *chickenshit*
with no music in it?   As deep
as I am now holding my self close,
recovering the rest of my life,

48

falling into the gap
of my fear and filling it
with the holy openness of my
heart, my pumping heart.

The Hospital of Lies

My grandfather has been lying
three years in a hospital bed, diminishing.
When he is small enough
I swaddle him in a sheet, lift him
in my arms, carry him away.
I bear him along the dock
jutting into the low-tide mudflats, past
all the weeping people and people
shooting crap. They are all
swathed in white, newly
risen from their beds, immaculately
squatting in clusters in the mud.
Their dice click
against the keels of the dry boats.
Nobody looks up, everybody
watches; nobody cares,
everyone wants to take him from me.
I lay him myself
finally in the mud at the end
and sit down beside him,
waiting for the tide to come undone.

2.

I sit on the floor of the hospital
where my brother is lying
over me in his newborn bed. I bide
my time, looking innocent.
My dice click against the white wall,
bounce back toward me, never
come up the same twice. I see the feet
of people who bend
over my brother and say he's beautiful.
I wait until everything else is empty,
then wrap him in a sheet
and lift him out of bed
with my claw. Scuttling, I bear him
across town, into my grandfather's garage.
While I'm hiding
us clustered in a high deep place
everyone comes together in the grease

stain spreading across the concrete floor.
All right I say, rising.
I give up; he's mine now.
I will be king and queen of the egg people
forever. Take him. I lift
his ovate body swaddled above me
and hurl it into the hard sea of people.
He should crack, he should shatter,
but he floats down and joins hands with the others.
They leave me with them
gone, again; I climb down
and sit, and watch my claw disappear
as I write my name in the grease with it.

3.

So I go into the lying hospital
my self. How else can I keep my people
from dying and being born,
from parading their don't-care
I-love-you in this muddy grease welcome
to the world? I am swaddled
in white. I lie down
and am rolled away on a table.
Wherever the others have gone
or come from will be where I am.
Whatever they have been given
to become themselves will be given
to me as well. All the people
in white will bend over me saying
We want you, we want you
gone. Hurry. There is nothing
here except everything. Take it.
Then the green men lean
over me, a black hole of rubber
closes on my face, I go backward
from 100 to absolute zero.
I forget to say this
isn't what I expected. I forget
how the king-and-queen wanted
to save his subjects and verve
—breadfather and greatbrother,
his killweather hardbreakers—how he wanted

to be fixed, to be perfect, so nobody
would have to be dead born dead, but

4.

I wake up anyway. My grandfather
is still alive in my head
where he's been buried for thirty years.
My brother drives a cowboy Cadillac
to work in Texas, while I throw him
still toward concrete into oblivion
forty years ago now. My voice
rasps sometimes; I crave
ice cream. All the nothing
that was given back I keep
as close to me as the greasy mudtumble
I play in until I die,
as close to me as the space
left in my throat, which I talk past.

A Bird

Even before he finished eating
Hansel's crumbs, he began to feel
bloated, his little craw
swelling with bread scraps
and moisture from the forest floor.
His body felt like something
else, a cell, an oven. His feathers
poked him like spiny
fingers, testing him for doneness.
His head ached.
The heat loosened his bones.
Still, he ate. When he swallowed
the last crumb the forest
vanished. A vestigial woman
on crutches lurched toward him
from all directions, composite
of hungers; her hair full of fire
was the only place
left to fly, so he nested in it,
quivering, heavy
with the strange lives molting
in his dreams—a boy and a girl
in flight, loping across open fields
toward a man bright with regret
and welcome, toward home.

Dressing

About five a.m. he hears dimly
hummingbirds in the lilac, senses
the sun leaking over the slats
of cream, plays a leapfrog
of sleepandwake nobody wins
until it's too late. He'd rather
climb back down where he can
be randy Jim Dandy of the sluice
gates in spring, taking
all comers. Nothing in fact
would please him more
than to be by dreams
exhausted to deeper dreaming.
But the thin membrane between
brains fogs up like a windowpane
he could write his name on
with his finger. Only a fading
static ekes through, not even
echoes of the living life.
So it means to wake up
and put on what he does, which
he likes as one could be said
to like the melon rind after the melon,
the husk of the self.

Regret

for Ellen Marie Stuart

I've heard we can talk about love
without talking about it,
but we don't talk about that.
We could climb out of this story
and into the next window—
scale the whole wall together—
and never get any closer
to learning how,
if that's what we wanted
to get closer to . . .
                the rough face
of brick against the cheek,
toes set into the seam of mortar,
the scraping knee, fingertips
measuring each brittle inch, edging
toward the clear panes rising. I could
help you in, or you could help me
in. We could stand there
in the new story, unfurnished space,
and remember scaling the whole wall.
We could tell our grandchildren about it,

                the rough face . . .
and they would begin, after trying
to listen, to stare into space
past us, our voices seeming
so much fine, pink dust drifting
toward quiet, a memory scaling away.
Maybe, when we trailed off
before we finished, one of them
would look back and, seeing the tears,
wonder if all old stories
have a happy ending.

I Can't Live Without You

I begin to die. I have been
dying all my life, of course,
but I begin
to die anyway. In my desperation
I discover a sexy woman
who wants to play. She takes
my bat and balls and fungoes me
out of the park. Flying high,
I pass the ex-poet John Keats
who has been bird hunting
and is on his way down.
John I say *This is the way to go.*
He says *When you begin to die*
time is the snake woman
who loves you better than all the world.
I hate my life he says *I hate being*
in my life. Afterward,
I stroke her head resting
against my belly. She hums
and I feel it in my veins, my pelvis,
my throat. Our music
shimmers for old John, for our
selves, for all hearts
fluttering in their twigs of blood.